40 Sensational
Sight Word
Games

BY JOAN NOVELLI

SCHOLASTIC
PROFESSIONAL BOOKS

NEW YORK • TORONTO • LONDON • AUCKLAND • SYDNEY
MEXICO CITY • NEW DELHI • HONG KONG • BUENOS AIRES

Special thanks to my bright and beautiful son, Dylan,

for consulting on this book.

He carefully read and considered each activity,

provided thoughtful feedback

(remembering his own sight word experiences just a few years ago),

and contributed a game of his own—

Simon Says Sight Words!

Look for it on page 23.

Cover design by Maria Lilja
Cover artwork by Nadine Bernard Wescott
Interior design by Kathy Massaro
Interior illustrations by James Graham Hale

ISBN: 0-439-30357-5
Copyright © 2002 by Joan Novelli.
Printed in U.S.A.

2 3 4 5 6 7 8 9 10   40   09 08 07 06 05 04 03 02

Contents

About This Book

Twinkle, twinkle, little star,
How I wonder what you are,
Up above the world so high,
Like a diamond in the sky,
Twinkle, twinkle, little star,
How I wonder what you are.

In six short lines, this familiar nursery rhyme gives children a chance to practice 12 different words that appear on the Dolch Basic Sight Word Vocabulary List—7 of them more than once. Sight words—such as *I, what, you, are, up, so*—are words that have been identified as appearing with high frequency in print. These are also the words that children use most frequently in their writing. Making these words part of a child's sight vocabulary means more fluent reading—and stronger spelling skills.

40 Sensational Sight Word Games has more than 40 quick, easy, and fun activities for including sight word lessons in your literacy program. These suggestions invite children to read, spell, write, draw, sing, mingle, move, and more, as they make these important words part of their reading and writing vocabulary. You'll find twists on classics such as Simon Says and Red Rover, Red Rover. (See pages 23 and 31.) There are other games to play, such as Rainstick Relay (see page 27), easy songs to learn and sing (see Sing a Song of Sight Words, page 35), pocket chart poems (see Go In and Out the Window, page 26), movement games (see Leaping Lilypads, page 24), tips for teaching sight words in your morning message (see Sight-Word-Building Morning Messages, page 25), how-tos for interactive sight word walls (see Grow a Sight Word Garden, page 40), school-home connections (see page 6), reproducible activity pages and patterns, and much more.

You can use the activities in any order, selecting those that suit your students' mood or your time frame. Most require little or no preparation, and few if any materials, which are most often everyday classroom supplies.

Guidelines for Teaching Sight Words

As you plan lessons to introduce sight words, keep in mind that many of these words are *irregular*—they don't follow the phonics rules that children may be learning. These words, such as those with *w* (*were, where, with, when*) and *th* (*the, them, then, this*), need to be learned, in the same ways that other words are learned—by looking at letters, sound-spelling patterns, and so on. Here are some general guidelines to keep in mind.

☆ Introduce the word, saying and spelling it.

☆ Read the word in a sentence, perhaps one that appears in a book you are sharing with students. Write the sentence on the chalkboard and underline the sight word, saying and spelling it again.

☆ Invite students to notice distinctive features of the word—for example, tall letters, double letters, and so on.

☆ Have children practice writing the word on mini whiteboards, in the air, at the chalkboard, in a writing journal, and so on.

☆ Add the word to a word wall. (See word wall suggestions, Sight Word Safari on page 20 and Bingo Word Wall on page 32.) Revisit the words often, encouraging students to notice the many new words they are learning.

✻.◎♡⚬.◎⚬.♡✻ Dolch Basic Sight Word Vocabulary List ✻.◎♡⚬.◎⚬.♡✻

Following are the 220 words that appear on the Dolch Basic Sight Word Vocabulary List—plus the word *nine*, which does not appear on the original list but has been added here because, in addition to the Dolch sight words *one, two, three, four, five, six, seven, eight,* and *ten*, it is a word children need to know. One hundred of these sight words are included on reproducible sight word cards. (See next page.)

a	best	do	done	gave	how	once	too	clean
been	cut	four	full	hold	live	right	when	find
come	for	her	him	like	old	start	ate	grow
five	he	know	let	of	read	today	can	it
has	keep	new	not	ran	some	were	far	me
jump	myself	please	pull	small	three	ask	got	out
must	pick	sing	six	this	well	call	into	say
over	she	there	they	wash	your	every	many	thank
seven	them	walk	warm	yes	around	going	open	under
the	use	work	write	any	buy	if	said	white
upon	wish	always	an	brown	eat	made	tell	because
why	again	black	both	draw	go	one	try	cold
about	better	does	don't	get	hurt	round	where	first
before	did	from	funny	hot	long	stop	away	had
could	found	here	his	little	on	together	carry	its
fly	help	laugh	light	off	ride	what	fast	much
have	kind	nine	now	read	soon	at	green	out
just	never	no	put	so	to	came	is	see
my	play	pretty	sleep	those	went	fall	may	that
own	show	sit	think	we	as	good	or	up
shall	then	these	was	you	by	in	saw	who
their	very	want	yellow	are	eight	make	ten	
us	with	would	and	but	goes	only	two	
will	all	am	bring	drink	I	run	which	
after	big	blue	down	give	look	take	be	

Making and Using the Top 100 Sight Word Cards

Pages 7 to 11 feature word cards that you can photocopy and cut apart. These "top" words, selected from the Dolch Basic Sight Word Vocabulary List, are among the most frequently used sight words. Cut apart and laminate the cards in advance of the activities so that they are readily available. Additional suggestions for using the word cards follow.

☆ Make several sets of sight word cards in advance. You may want to enlarge the cards first. Or write sight words on index cards and laminate them.

☆ Presort words you know you want to teach separately—for example, pull out words for teaching short-vowel sounds (such as *and, as, is, it, on, not*) or words for teaching initial consonants (such as *do, did, down*).

☆ Keep manageable lists of the sight words handy for children to use. My Sight Words (see page 12) has space for recording two sets of 20 words each, with room for children to practice writing each word they need to learn. Write in the words you want each child to learn, or make a master and photocopy a class set. Children can "test" themselves with this page, checking off the words they can read and highlighting those they need to practice.

Making School-Home Connections

Encourage your students' success with sight words by involving families in learning. Start by sending home the sight word cards on pages 7 to 11 with the letter on page 13. Children can cut apart the words and store them in a resealable bag at home, then practice reading and spelling the words with a family member. Pages 14–16 feature additional sight-word-building activities for children to take home and try with their families. There's space on these pages to write in ten sight words that you want students to learn. You might fill in these words before photocopying the class set, or tailor the lists to meet the needs of each child. Use page 18 to brainstorm with students their own Top 10 Ways to Practice Sight Words. Then photocopy the page for children to take home to use with their families.

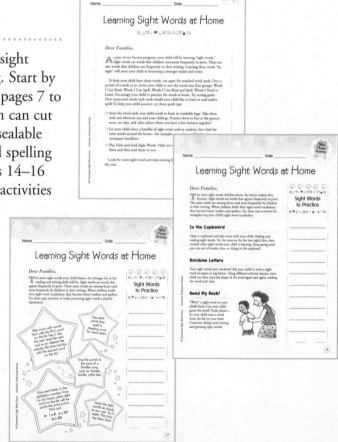

me	them	how	when	with
he	we	your	who	will
she	us	you	what	which
I	they	our	why	where

Name _____ Date _____

My Sight Words

· ·

Which words do you know? Check the ones you can read. Highlight the ones you need to practice! Practice spelling, writing, and reading them.

Sight Words	My Turn

Sight Words	My Turn

40 Sensational Sight Word Games   Scholastic Professional Books

Name _____ Date _____

Learning Sight Words at Home

Dear Families,

As part of our literacy program, your child will be learning "sight words." Sight words are words that children encounter frequently in print. These are also words that children use frequently in their writing. Learning these words "by sight" will assist your child in becoming a stronger reader and writer.

To help your child learn these words, cut apart the attached word cards. Over a period of a week or so, invite your child to sort the words into four groups: Words I Can Read, Words I Can Spell, Words I Can Read and Spell, Words I Need to Learn. Encourage your child to practice the words at home. Try setting goals: How many new words each week would your child like to learn to read and/or spell? To help your child practice, try these quick tips:

☆ Store the word cards your child needs to learn in resealable bags. Take them with you wherever you and your child go. Practice them in line at the grocery store, on trips, and other places where you have a few minutes together!

☆ Let your child select a handful of sight word cards at random, then find the same words around the house—for example, on packages of food or in newspaper headlines.

☆ Play Hide-and-Seek Sight Words. Hide ten word cards. Let your child find them and then read them to you.

Look for more sight word activities coming home with your child throughout the year.

Sincerely,

Name _____ Date _____

Learning Sight Words at Home

Dear Families,

Learning sight words helps children become stronger readers and writers. Sight words—such as *him, her, an,* and *all*—are words that children encounter frequently in print. They are also among the words children use most frequently in their writing. One of our literacy goals is to help children learn to read and spell these words automatically. Here are some at-home activities for building your child's sight word vocabulary.

Sing a Song of Sight Words

Practice sight words by singing them to a familiar tune or making up your own. If you run out of words before you get to the end of the song, just start at the top of the list again. Some songs to try include "Twinkle, Twinkle, Little Star" and "Row, Row, Row Your Boat."

Jump on It!

Copy sight words on index cards (one word per card). Make a second set of the same words. Scatter one set faceup on the floor, leaving about a foot between each card. Place the other set in a stack facedown. Turn over the first card in the stack. Have your child read the word (offer help as needed) and then jump on the corresponding card on the floor. Turn over the next card and have your child read it and jump to that word. Continue until your child has jumped on all of the words. Mix up the cards and play again!

Which Word Wins?

Sit with your child and look at a newspaper to see just how often sight words pop up in print. Ask your child to choose a sight word from the list and an article from the paper. Look for the word together. Highlight and count the word each time it appears. Try the same thing with a second sight word. Which word appears more often?

Sight Words to Practice

_____

_____

_____

_____

_____

_____

_____

_____

_____

40 Sensational Sight Word Games Scholastic Professional Books

Name _____ Date _____

Learning Sight Words at Home

Dear Families,

The more sight words children know, the better readers they become. Sight words are words that appear frequently in print. The same words are among those used most frequently by children in their writing. When children build their sight word vocabulary, they become better readers and spellers. Try these easy activities for strengthening your child's sight word vocabulary.

In the Cupboard

Open a cupboard and take turns with your child, finding and reading sight words. Try the ones on the list (see right) first, then include other sight words your child is learning. Keep going until you run out of words, time, or things in the cupboard.

Rainbow Letters

Turn sight words into rainbows! Ask your child to write a sight word on paper in big letters. Using different-colored crayons, your child can then trace around the word again and again, reading the word each time.

Read My Back!

"Write" a sight word on your child's back. Can your child guess the word? Trade places— let your child trace a word from the list on your back. Continue taking turns tracing and guessing sight words.

Sight Words to Practice

_____

_____

_____

_____

_____

_____

_____

_____

Name _____ Date _____

Learning Sight Words at Home

Dear Families,

The more sight words your child knows, the stronger his or her reading and writing skills will be. Sight words are words that appear frequently in print. These same words are among those used most frequently by children in their writing. When children build their sight word vocabulary, they become better readers and spellers. Try these easy activities for strengthening your child's sight word vocabulary.

On the Run

The next time you're going somewhere with your child, play a sight word game. It's easy—just have your child find as many sight words as he or she can on billboards, signs, and so on. If you don't have a sight word list with you, invite your child to read the "little" words. You can play this game in a car, on a walk, even in line at the grocery store!

Spill a Sight Word

Copy sight words onto small cards. (You can cut index cards in quarters or cut sturdy paper into pieces.) Place the word cards in an empty container, such as a tall plastic tumbler or an empty tennis ball can. Invite your child to shake the container, spill out the words, and read the ones that fall faceup. Give each word your child reads a score that is equal to the number of letters in the word. Record the total, then place the remaining words back in the can and shake and spill again. Add the total to the first score. Play until your child has spilled and read all of the words.

I'm Thinking of...

Play a game of "I'm thinking of…" One player starts by giving a clue about one of the sight words—for example, "I'm thinking of a word that starts like *horse* and has three letters." The other player looks at the list and tries to identify the word. (*his*)

Sight Words to Practice

_____

_____

_____

_____

_____

_____

_____

_____

_____

40 Sensational Sight Word Games   Scholastic Professional Books

Name _____ Date _____

Learning Sight Words at Home

Dear Families,

The more sight words your child knows, the stronger his or her reading and writing skills will be. Sight words are words that appear frequently in print. These same words are among those used most frequently by children in their writing. When children build their sight word vocabulary, they become better readers and spellers. Try these easy activities to make practicing sight words a playful experience!

Skip-count with words: Start with the first word on the list. Say it, skip the next, read the next, and so on. Repeat the activity, this time starting with the second word on the list.

Say each word, then spell it, clapping once for each letter.

Sing the words to the tune of a familiar song, such as "Twinkle, Twinkle, Little Star."

Give each letter in the alphabet a number from 1 to 26. Guess which sight word on the list will be worth the most points. Find out!

is i = 9 s = 20
is = 29

Read the sight words as slowly as you can. Try it again. This time say them fast!

Sight Words to Practice

Name _____ Date _____

Top-10 Ways to Practice Sight Words

Dear Families,

Here's a countdown of our top-ten favorite ways to practice sight words. Try them at home to build your child's sight word vocabulary.

10 _____

9 _____

8 _____

7 _____

6 _____

5 _____

4 _____

3 _____

2 _____

And our number one favorite way to practice sight words is...

1 _____

40 Sensational Sight Word Games   Scholastic Professional Books

Buzz!

This game puts the fun in flashcards—reinforcing sight words and giving children a chance to stretch their legs and arms at the same time.

1 Write sight words on index cards.

2 Add cards (the same size) that say "Buzz!" (You can copy and cut apart the "Buzz!" cards on page 49 and glue them to index cards.)

3 Shuffle the word cards, then gather students together to play. If they're sitting in a circle, be sure they leave enough room between them so that they can move around when the time comes.

4 Flash the first word. If it's a sight word, have students read it. If it says "Buzz!" have everyone say the word and then jump up and buzz about. Gather your bees back together by saying "Back to the hive!" Continue with the next card. (You might have children read the words as a group the first time through, then individually a second time.)

Tip

Your students will enjoy making their own versions of the game to play, substituting other movement words for "Buzz!" Some to try include "High Five" (with everyone "high-fiving" their neighbor), "Bunny Hop" (children get up and hop), and "Bug Boogie" (children wiggle about like their favorite insects).

Sight Word Soup

A pot brimming with colorful noodles makes a fun prop for building sight word vocabulary.

1 Write sight words on large noodles. Rigatoni works well. Use brightly colored permanent markers.

2 Fill a pot with the noodles. Provide a plastic ladle and some bowls.

3 Invite children to visit the sight word soup pot in pairs and scoop out a bowl of words for each other. Let them read the words on their noodles aloud, and make a list to reinforce spelling.

Sight Word Safari

A walk around the school provides all sorts of real-life reading opportunities, including many that will let students see just how often people use sight words.

1 Gather children together for a walk around the school. Ask them to be on the lookout for sight words. Review words on your sight word wall or chart in preparation.

2 Take a clipboard, paper, and pencil with you to record words children find. Let children take turns carrying the clipboard and recording the words.

3 Back in the classroom, review the words students recognized. What sight words did they see in the nurse's office? In the cafeteria? In other places?

Squirt and Spell

Shaving cream on a desk makes a fun place to practice spelling sight words. Try this activity at the end of the day for shiny desks the next day.

1 Give each child a squirt of shaving cream on his or her desk. Let children use their hands to spread out the shaving cream over the desk surface. This will also give them a chance to just have fun feeling the shaving cream.

2 Explain that you are going to say a sight word and that you want children to try writing the word with their finger in the shaving cream.

3 Take a walk around to check children's spelling, then have them wipe their words away and get ready for a new word.

4 When you're ready to wrap up, children can use paper towels or sponges to wipe away the shaving cream. Now you've got stronger spellers and clean desks!

Tip

You may wish to also hold up a sight word card so that students can use it as a reference in spelling the word on their desks. Or let them try the word twice—once while looking at the card, then wiping the word away and spelling it a second time without looking.

Magic Wand Words

Tip

Set up several sight word baskets (with wands) so that students can use them on their own or in small groups. You can also send home the baskets and wands for children to play with family members.

Sight words written on slips of paper invite children to roam the room to find more.

1 Write sight words on slips of paper. (Or copy and cut apart the word cards on pages 7–11.)

2 Make a magic wand: Cut out a tagboard star shape. Dab glue on both sides of the star and sprinkle with glitter. Glue the star to one end of a dowel and tie on some curly ribbon.

3 Place the words in a box or basket, and gather children in a circle. Start by selecting one word from the basket. Read the word aloud and show it to students. Tell them that you're now going to find the same word somewhere in the room. Check posters, book covers, and other readily available sources for the word. When you find the same word, use the wand to point it out. Add a flourish for emphasis.

4 Pass the wand and the words to a volunteer, who repeats the procedure. Continue until each child has had a chance to find a word. Return the words to the basket for another time.

◉ Tip ◉

For a cooperative version, have students play to empty the can within a specified amount of time they agree on—for example, five minutes. Children who get an "Oh, No!" card still have to put back their cards, but classmates will hang on to theirs for the end goal of emptying the can together. In the spirit of teamwork, you might say that children who get stuck on a word can ask either a child to their left or right for help.

Oh, No!

In this fast-paced game, students take turns selecting sight word cards from a container. They keep each word they can read. But it's back to the beginning if they take a word card that says "Oh, No!" How many words will they get before the can is empty?

1 Select a group of sight words to practice. Make three to four times as many cards as you have students. (You can use duplicates of words.) Copy and laminate those word cards (see pages 7–11), or use cards you have made in advance.

2 Place the word cards in an large, empty oatmeal container. Add a few extra word cards that say "Oh, No!"

3 Gather children in a circle. Begin by selecting a word card at random. Read the word on the card. If students agree that you have read the word correctly, you get to keep the card.

4 Pass the container to the child on your right. That child selects a card at random and keeps it if he or she can read it. The game continues in this way, with children keeping cards for words they read. If a child gets an "Oh, No!" card, he or she must put back the word cards and begin again.

5 Play until there are no more cards in the container. Children can count the cards they have, though you'll want to keep the emphasis off who has the most.

Simon Says Sight Words!

This twist on a favorite game strengthens listening skills, too.

1 Write sight words on index cards, punch two holes in the top of each, and string with yarn to make necklaces. Give one to each child. (It's okay if some children have the same word.)

2 Gather children in a seated circle, or have them sit at their desks.

3 Review the game Simon Says, then explain that in this version you will call out sight words and name an action. Anyone who is wearing the words you call performs the action. Here's an example of what you might say: "Simon says, *as, and, at* shake your neighbor's hand." or "Simon says, *if, I, in* hop on one foot ten times."

4 Play until every child has had plenty of chances to participate. By always including the words "Simon says," children participate each time you call out words and name an action. This way, nobody is "out" and everyone has fun.

Sight Word Snake

This human snake grows with each new sight word children recognize.

1 Start by holding up a sight word card and inviting a child to read it. Have that child hold up the next card and ask another child to read it. That child gets up and takes the first child's hand.

2 Continue, with each successive child holding up a word card and inviting a classmate to read it. Each child who reads a word connects to the "snake" by holding the last child's hand.

3 Keep going until every child is part of the snake. Let your class snake "slither" around the classroom or school to celebrate the sight words learned.

Leaping Lilypads

Children get to stretch their legs as they practice sight words with this game.

1 Copy sight words onto index cards (one word per card). Make a second set of the same words. Tape one set of words to tagboard cut into lilypad shapes (one word per lilypad).

2 Scatter the lilypads faceup on the floor, leaving about a foot between each, and tape in place securely. Place the other set of word cards facedown in a stack.

3 Turn over the first card in the stack, and have the first player read the word and then jump on the corresponding card on the floor. (Offer assistance as needed so that every child is successful.)

4 Turn over the next card, and have the child read it and jump to that word. Continue until the child has jumped on all of the words.

5 Mix up the cards and let another child take a turn.

Sight-Word-Building Morning Messages

Here are five ways to turn your morning message or daily letter into a sight-word-building activity.

1 Greet students with a morning message that invites them to read a list of sight words (five or so), write the words on the chart paper, and sign their names.

2 In your morning message, invite children to be sight word detectives, challenging them to find as many sight words as they can.

3 Read the morning message with children. Say the sight words that appear in the message, one at a time. Let children take turns highlighting them.

4 Write your morning message, but leave blank lines where sight words belong. Try to leave one for each student. End your message by asking children to fill in one missing word each. Read the completed message together.

5 Introduce a new group of sight words in the morning message. Ask children to tell one way they'd like to practice them. They can write their responses on the morning message chart paper or share them in your class meeting.

25

Go In and Out the Window

The title of this familiar song has six words—five of them sight words! Use the song to have fun reinforcing sight word vocabulary while letting children move about.

1 Write the words to "Go In and Out the Window" on chart paper. The first three verses, along with suggested movements, follow. Your students will have fun making up more.

Go in and out the window,
Go in and out the window,
Go in and out the window,
As we have done before.

(Children are in a circle. One child weaves in and out of the circle, alternately going in front of and behind the others.)

Now stand and face your partner,
Now stand and face your partner,
Now stand and face your partner,
As we have done before.

(Children turn and face the child to their left.)

Now follow me to London,
Now follow me to London,
Now follow me to London,
As we have done before.

(Children follow a "leader" around the room, everyone single file.)

2 Sing the song, using the movements suggested or making up your own. (You can also just sing the first verse again and again, and let children take turns weaving in and out of the circle.)

3 Let children take turns saying sight words they know and highlighting them on the chart paper.

Spill a Sight Word

Combine literacy and math skills with this fast-paced game.

1 Make a set of sight word cards. Place the word cards in an empty container, such as an empty tennis ball container. Make several sets of these.

2 Divide the class into small groups. Give each group a word card container. Explain how to play:

☆ Have the first player shake the container and then spill out the words and read the ones that fall faceup. Give each word that is read a score that is equal to the number of letters in the word.

☆ Record the total, then place the remaining words (those that the player didn't read, including those that fell facedown) back in the can and pass the container to the next player.

☆ The next player shakes the container, spills the words, adds up the score, and the game continues. Play until all the words have been read. What's the group total?

Tip

This game works best with groups of two to four children, so that no player has to wait too long to take another turn.

Rainstick Relay

This game uses a rainstick to exercise students' sight word recognition skills.

1 Gather students together to share a poem on chart paper or a big book (set on an easel).

2 Revisit the poem or story, this time having students be on the lookout for sight words. Call out a sight word you want students to find, turn the rainstick over, and pass it to a child. Have that child find and point to the word before the "rainstorm" ends and then call out another sight word, turn over the rainstick, and pass it to another child.

3 This child finds and points to the sight word before the rainstorm ends, and the relay continues until everyone has had a chance to pass the rainstick. If you run out of words first, go back to the beginning or share another poem or story.

Tip

If you don't have a rainstick, check with the music teacher or another colleague who might have one to loan.

Play-Clay Shape and Spell

Put a kinesthetic spin on teaching sight words by mixing up a batch of play clay. (See recipe, below.)

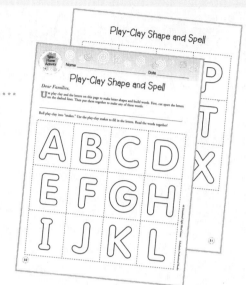

1 Use the computer to print out sight words in large, outline form. Laminate each sheet of words, then cut apart to make word outline cards (one word per card).

2 Invite children to help you mix up a batch of no-cook play clay. They can take turns measuring and mixing the dough and then dividing it into portions for each child.

3 Give each child some word cards. Have children roll their clay to make "snakes." Then have them use the snakes to fill in the outline of each word.

4 When children have had enough time to fill in their words, have them switch cards and make new words.

Make Play Clay

Here's an easy no-cook recipe for play clay.

☆ Mix 2 cups white flour with 1 cup salt, 4 tablespoons vegetable oil, and 1 teaspoon alum.

☆ Add water, a little at a time, until the mixture is the right consistency (about 1 cup).

☆ Knead in food coloring as desired, pulling sections of the dough apart to make batches of different colors.

☆ Store play clay in a sealed container.

Peekaboo Word-Finder Window

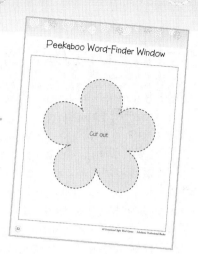

A playful word-finder window turns learning sight words into a game of I Spy.

1 Give each child a copy of the word-finder window pattern on page 52. Have children glue the pattern onto tagboard, cut out the window on the dashed lines, and decorate the frame. Glitter is always a welcome addition.

2 Ask children to tape their window to a craft stick to make a handle.

3 Let children use their peekaboo word finders when reading poems, big books, and so on, with the class. As you read, stop periodically and say, "I spy the word [insert word here]" and have a volunteer locate the word and place the word finder over the word so that it is framed by the window.

Letters Line Up

Children arrange themselves to spell sight words. How fast can they spell them all?

1 Choose a set of sight words to practice. Write them on index cards, one letter per card. Punch a hole in the left and right corner of each card and tie on a length of yarn or ribbon to make a necklace. Then make a second set of cards on which you've written the entire word.

2 Give each child a necklace. Say a word and hold up the corresponding card. Have children who can help spell that word with their necklace letters come to the front of the room and arrange themselves in order. (More than one child may have some of the letters. Reassure children that they will each get to use their letters.)

3 Have the first group of children remain standing to spell the word. Say and display a second word and have corresponding children come up to arrange themselves to spell that word. Continue until all children are part of a word.

4 Let children in each group lead a cheer to say and spell their word—for example, "Give me a *p*! Give me an *l*! Give me an *e*! Give me an *a*! Give me an *s*! Give me another *e*! What's that spell? *Please!*"

Beep!

Children use syntax and conventions of language to guess which sight words you're leaving out of a read-aloud story.

1 Choose a picture book to read aloud.

2 Tell children that whenever they hear the word *Beep!* it means you've left out a word. They need to guess what the word is.

3 Read the story a second time, this time letting children chime in on as many sight words as they know.

Red Rover, Red Rover

This twist on a traditional game is just right when students have some extra energy to expend.

1 Prepare to play by making a word card necklace for each child. For each necklace, write "It" on one side of an index card. On the other side, write any other sight word you wish to include. Punch a hole in the top left and right corners of the card, and then tie on a length of yarn or ribbon to make a necklace.

2 Find a large space in which to play. Mark two lines at opposite ends of the space.

3 Give each child a word necklace. Invite a volunteer to be "It." Have this child turn his or her necklace so that the word *It* faces out. Have everyone else wear the necklaces so that the other sight words face out.

4 Have the child who is "It" stand in the center of the space. Have the other children stand behind one of the lines.

5 To begin, have that child call out "Red Rover, Red Rover, let anyone with [fill in a sight word] come over!" The child wearing the necklace with that word on it must try to run to the line at the opposite end without being tagged by "It."

6 If the player is tagged, he or she turns the word card over so that it says "It" and joins the child in the middle. The game continues, with the original "It" calling another player: "Red Rover, Red Rover, let anyone with [fill in a new sight word] come over!"

7 As more children are tagged, it will be increasingly difficult for players to get to the opposite end. When everyone has been called and is either safe or "It," let children trade necklaces and play again.

Bingo Word Wall

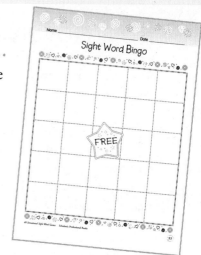

Bingo is always a fun way to reinforce learning. Use the blank Bingo board on page 53 to play Sight Word Bingo with students. For a setup that makes it easy to play anytime, create a sight-word wall using Velcro®. Just attach Velcro to the back of the word cards and to the wall. This makes it easy for children to fill in their Bingo boards, and to take the words off the wall to play.

1 Give each child a copy of the Sight Word Bingo board. Provide children with dried beans or other objects to fill in their Bingo boards.

2 Ask children to fill in each square on their game boards with a sight word from the word wall.

3 Remove words from the word wall and place them in a bag or box.

4 Choose a word, show it to students, and read it. Children who have that word on their boards place a marker in that space.

5 Play until one child gets five across, down, or diagonally. Let that child read the words. Continue playing until everyone has five in a row, or start a new game.

What's My Word? Lineup Game

Practice sight words anytime children have to line up for lunch or other activities outside the classroom. This line-up game reinforces listening skills, too.

1 Make a list of sight words. Put the same sight word cards in a can.

2 A few minutes before children need to line up to go to an activity, invite them to each pick one card.

3 Read the sight words one at a time, having children line up as they hear their words called.

4 When everyone's in line, pass the can to collect the words for the next time.

Pick a Partner

Use this quick matching game anytime you need children to pick a partner for an activity.

1 Make two identical sets of sight word cards, so there is one card for each child. Place the word cards in a can.

2 When children need to choose partners, have them each choose a card from the can.

3 Ask children to find the child who has the same word card. Have partners sit down together when they make a match and practice reading their word.

4 When everyone has a partner, let each pair of children take a turn reading their words aloud.

In the Hat

A magician's hat and wand invite children to practice sight words again and again.

1 Make a magician's hat by cutting a black tagboard brim to fit around the top of an oatmeal box that you've painted black. Make a magic wand by cutting out a star and decorating it with glitter, gluing it to a dowel or ruler, then tying on curly ribbon.

2 Copy and cut apart the sight word cards on pages 7–11. Place them in the hat.

3 Wave the wand over the hat and make up a chant—for example, *Abracadabra. Abracadee. What will I pull from this hat? Watch and see!* Pull a word out of the hat (better if you have a black hankerchief to obscure the act). Read it.

4 Pass around the hat. Let children make up their own chants and then pull out a word and read it.

Glow-in-the-Dark Word Stars

When you write sight words on stars with glow-in-the-dark markers, your classroom will light up with all the words students know.

1 Enlist students' help in cutting out stars from tagboard. (Provide several templates for them to pass around.) Make the stars large enough to write a word in letters that children can read from a distance.

2 On the stars, write sight words that children learn, using glow-in-the-dark markers or paint.

3 Set the stars aside until you have at least ten. Then, when your students are out of the room for lunch or a special, punch a hole at the top, tie on a length of yarn, and hang from the ceiling. Surprise them with the lights off when they arrive. Watch their faces light up when they see their stars shine!

Word Star Template

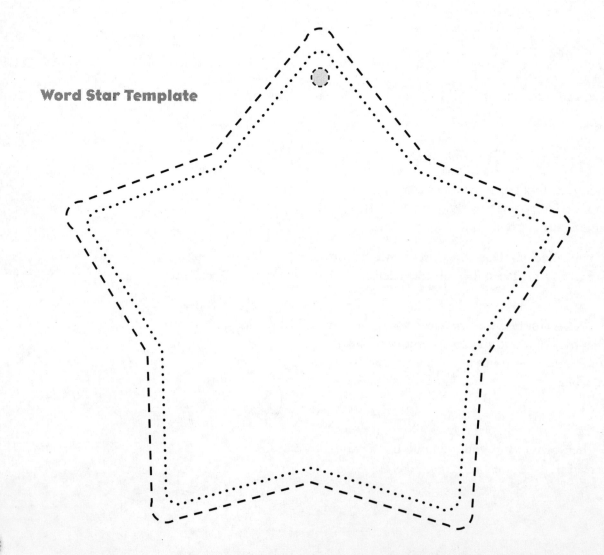

Sing a Song of Sight Words

Sing sight words to the tune of the ABC song.

1 Write 26 sight words you want to reinforce (or fewer, but write some words more than once to equal 26 words) on sentence strips. Trim and place in a pocket chart.

2 Use a pointer to direct children's attention to each word as they sing it to the tune of the ABC song.

3 Try singing sight words to other famliar tunes—for example, "Row, Row, Row Your Boat" and "London Bridge Is Falling Down."

Tip

This makes a great morning circle activity. As children become familiar with the activity, they will enjoy selecting words to place in the pocket chart and using the pointer as the class sings.

I'm Thinking of...

Play this game to reinforce sight word spelling and sounds. You'll want to display the sight words you are teaching on a word wall or chart.

1 Start the game by saying "I'm thinking of a sight word that starts with the same sound as [say a word that starts with the same sound as your target sight word] and has [number of letters].

2 Invite children to write down the word when they think they know it.

3 Continue playing, changing the types of clues you give. For example, you could say, "I'm thinking of a word that starts with the same letter as Becky's name, but it has two fewer letters." (The sight word *big* would fit this description.)

4 When children are familiar with the procedure, let them take turns providing the clues.

Mingle and Match

Reinforce word recognition with an activity that lets children practice writing their names, too.

1 Write sight words on a grid, with as many squares as you have students. Photocopy a class set.

2 Write the same words on index cards. Punch holes at the top left and right corners and string with yarn to make necklaces.

3 Give each child a necklace to wear and a grid.

4 Have children mingle, looking for the child whose necklace matches each word on the grid. (Matches do not need to be made in order of words on the grid.) Children sign their names to each other's grids as they visit, with both children saying and spelling the word.

5 When everyone has completed the grid, have children stand up and read their words one at a time.

Sight Word Search

Use the template on page 54 to make fun sight word search games. Looking for sight words among a grid of letters will reinforce word recognition and spelling skills.

1 Write a set of sight words on the grid, wherever you like.

2 Fill in empty spaces with random letters.

3 Give copies to children and challenge them to find as many sight words from a given list as they can.

Make Sight Word Mats

Children have easy access to sight words with this placemat. Send it home to encourage practice at the dinner table!

1 Give each child a sheet of large drawing paper and a set of sight word cards. (See pages 7–11.) Guide children in marking off a border of about one inch around the perimeter of the paper.

2 Have children cut apart the sight word cards and glue them onto the drawing paper. They don't have to be in straight lines. In fact, children may prefer to have fun with the placement of the words, using them to create shapes, even pictures.

3 Let children color a border, using solid colors, patterns, or pictures. They can also color around the words or use very light colors over them.

4 Laminate the placemats and send them home with a list of suggestions for practicing sight words. (See the take-home activities on pages 13–18 for ideas.)

Eggs in a Basket
(and a Surprise in One!)

The plastic eggs that are often available at craft and grocery stores in the spring are great to have on hand for all sorts of special activities. Here's one that reinforces sight word spelling.

1 Cut apart sight words letter by letter and place the letters for each word in an egg. Do this for about a dozen eggs.

2 Place the eggs and a list of the sight words in a basket.

3 Let children take the basket to their desks to work with the sight words. Have them "crack" each egg, one at a time, and arrange the letters to spell a word. Have them check their spelling using the list provided.

4 When children have cracked all the eggs and spelled all the words, have them return the letters to the eggs and put the eggs back in the basket for the next child.

5 For a special surprise, fill one egg with a treat such as a sticker. (When each child gets ready to return the eggs to the basket, he or she can get a new treat from you to put in the special egg.)

Shake, Read, and Write

This might be about the only time you'll find yourself recommending that children shake an egg carton.

1 Gather several empty egg cartons. Write a sight word in the bottom of each section in the egg cartons and a number from 1 to 12. Add a dried bean to each carton, close the tops, and you're ready to play this cooperative game.

2 Divide the class into small groups. Give each an egg carton, paper, and a pencil. Have children in each group take turns shaking the carton, then opening it and reading the word in the section that the dried bean landed in.

3 Have the player write the word and number for that word on the record sheet and pass the carton to the next player. This player again shakes the carton and reads the word, then records the word and score and adds the two numbers together.

4 Players continue until the group scores 50. How many words did it take? Let each group play again, and compare the two scores. Did it take more or fewer words the second time?

Tip

Ask children to bring in from home empty egg cartons. Write a sight word in each section, add a dried bean, and send the carton home again for children to play with family members.

Tip

If you run out of room in the garden and need space for new words, "pick" the flowers in one group and come up with a new flower shape together.

Grow a Sight Word Garden

This is no ordinary word wall. Watch it bloom along with your students as they master new sight words.

1 Use the patterns on page 55 to cut out flower shapes from brightly colored nonfading construction paper. (Or copy them and let children color them.)

2 Involve children in mapping out a garden on the wall. Plan a space for each kind of flower—roses, daffodils, and so on.

3 Assign a flower to each group of sight words you teach. As children learn the words, write them on flowers and "plant" them on the wall.

4 Let children fill in the garden with their own additions, such as cutouts of ladybugs, birds, and butterflies. Practice "reading" the garden, going from flower bed to flower bed. You can attach Velcro to the wall and to the backs of the flowers so that children can "pick" the flowers as they read them (then return them to the wall for another child).

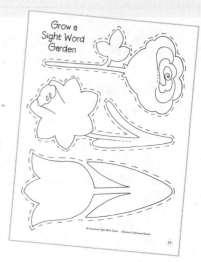

Rhyming Word Builders

Use sight words to introduce or reinforce word families. Choose a sight word that contains a phonogram you want to teach—for example, the sight word *that* contains the phonogram *-at* and can be used to teach words such as *pat, hat, cat, sat,* and *mat.* Play a rhyming word-building game to form words that contain the target phonogram.

1 Use clean, dry milk cartons to make blocks. (Push the top in to square off the box. Tape it in place.) Cut out squares of paper that are the same size as one side of a block. Write the sight word on one square and tape it to a block.

2 Read the word with children. Write it on the board and underline the phonogram. Say that sound with children and spell it. Place the block on a table (or the floor).

3 Write the phonogram on additional squares of paper, leaving room at the beginning for the initial consonant, consonant blend, or digraph. Tape the word squares to blocks, one per block.

4 Invite children to suggest new words that belong to this family. Help them add the letters to the blocks to spell the words. Together, say and spell the words. Let children add each completed block to the one before to build a tower of words! How high can they go?

Tip

Other sight word/phonogram pairs and words to teach follow. Check the Dolch Basic Sight Word Vocabulary List (see page 5) for more.

made (*-ade*)
way (*-ay*)
can (*-an*)
like (*-ike*)
look (*-ook*)
stop (*-op*)

41

Word Construction Site

The reproducible activity on page 56 challenges children to build sight words—one brick at a time.

1 Give each child a copy of the reproducible page. Ask children what they think the crane is holding. (*letters to complete the words that the bricks on the building spell*)

2 Do one word together. Explain that children need to consider all choices carefully—there are extra letters and they need to build all of the words.

3 Let children continue building the words on their own or in small groups. Review them together. For a fun followup, let children trace the crane and building and make new activity sheets to share.

Catch a Word!

This beach ball game will become a favorite way to practice reading and spelling sight words.

1 Tape strips of masking tape to the stripes on a beach ball. Write sight words on the strips.

2 Gather children in a circle, leaving an arm's length or so between each child.

3 Toss the ball to a child and have that child read one of the sight words that his or her hand is on. You then spell the word that he or she read.

4 Have the child who caught the ball toss it to another child. That child reads a word and the one who tossed it spells it.

5 The game continues until everyone has had a least one chance to read and spell a word. (Remind children to toss the ball to someone who hasn't had a turn.) Children who would like assistance reading or spelling might be invited to ask a neighbor to the left or right for a clue.

Sight Word Sandwiches

Tip

Choose sight words from the list of the top 100 words on pages 7 to 11, or augment your selection with additional sight words from the list on page 5.

What's for lunch? Sight words are a popular choice at this sandwich shop.

1 Cut shapes from different-colored construction paper to represent sandwich makings. For example, different-sized circles can represent peanut butter (cut from light brown), jam (blue), lettuce (green), tomato (red), cucumber (white with green marker border), ham (pink), turkey (beige), cream cheese (white), egg (yellow inside white). Cut strips of paper for pickles (green) and bacon (brown). Cut rings for peppers (green) and onions (white). Cut additional rectangles and circles to represent various breads (light brown ovals for rye, white or light brown circles for pita, long white ovals for French bread, and so on). Invite children to think of their own sandwich ingredients and to help cut out shapes to represent them.

2 Write sight words on the different shapes. Create a menu on chart paper, grouping each kind of sandwich ingredient together (breads, vegetables, cheeses, and so on).

3 Model the activity by asking a child to order a sandwich. Remind the child to include a bread and at least one filling. Make the sandwich, placing the filling shapes in between the bread shapes. Place the sandwich on a paper plate and give it to your young customer.

4 Have the child read the words in the sandwich, requesting help from the chef if desired.

5 Invite two volunteers to be the new chef and customer, ordering and making a new sandwich, then reading the sight word on each ingredient. Continue, letting children take turns at the sandwich shop.

43

Zoom!

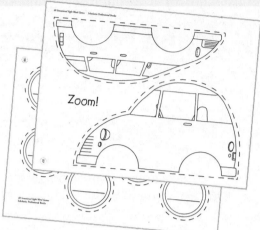

How many cars can crowd the highway of this interactive display? As many as the sight words your students learn!

1 Make multiple copies of the car and wheel patterns on pages 57 and 58. Let children color them and cut them out.

2 Display a roll of bulletin board paper in the hallway outside the classroom. Let children use markers or paint to turn the paper into a highway, adding yellow and white lines, even highway signs.

3 Ask students to suggest a sight word they know. Write the word on a wheel and add it to a car. Write a second word on another wheel to complete the car. Glue the car to the highway.

4 As children learn new sight words, write them on wheels. Glue wheels by twos on new cars and add them to the highway. Watch the cars line up as students learn more and more words. Can they make the highway stretch from one end of the hallway to the other?

5 Revisit the display often, letting students "take a drive" down the highway. Watch them zoom through all those words they know!

Bounce It, Say It, Catch It, Spell It

This outdoor game invites children to learn words as they bounce a ball to one another.

1 Use chalk to draw a large square (about five feet on a side) on a safe area of blacktop. Divide that square into four equal, smaller squares.

2 Write sight words inside each smaller square, leaving room for a child to stand in the square.

3 Have three children volunteer to stand in the squares with you to model the game. Bounce a ball (one bounce) to one child. As you bounce the ball, say one of the words in that child's square.

4 As that child catches the ball, he or she spells the word, then bounces the ball to another child and says a sight word in that child's square. That child spells the new word, bounces the ball to another child, says a new sight word, and so on.

5 Continue, with children bouncing the ball and saying and spelling words, until it's time to give a new group of children a turn.

◎ Tip ◎

Remind children that if they get stuck spelling a word, they can look at the words in their squares for help.

Silly (and Serious) Pocket Chart Sentence Makers

Your students will enjoy working together to build silly and serious sentences with sight words in a pocket chart.

1 Place sight word cards in a pocket chart. Make sure you have enough function words. (Add to the list of top 100 words by choosing other words from the Dolch Basic Sight Word Vocabulary List on page 5, too.)

2 Bring children together to model the activity. Choose several sight words that you can use to make a sentence and arrange them in order one by one. Read the sentence with children. Have them suggest words to make a new sentence. Place them in order in the pocket chart.

3 Let children work in pairs or small groups to make more sentences—silly or serious. Encourage them to read their sentences aloud to you.

Street Sign Sight Word Map

On this map, children make their way from one place to another by reading sight word street signs.

1 Give each child a copy of the map on page 59. Let children color their maps, being careful not to obscure words with dark colors.

2 Copy the car, bike, people, pet, and truck markers on page 60 and give one to each child. Have children color their markers.

3 Ask children to place their markers at the Stop sign on Brown Parkway, facing the Walk/Don't Walk sign. Then share the following story. Have students move their markers as indicated by the directions to get from start to finish. Does everyone end up at the same place?

> You're going to a friend's house. Where does she live? Follow the directions to find out. Turn right on Brown Parkway. Take a left on Green Fly Drive. Go slow; you're going to make the first right on See Saw Street. Oops. Wrong turn! Go back out to Green Fly Drive and take a right. At the Stop sign, take another right on Small Circle. Your friend's house is the first house on the left!

4 Have children continue to play with the maps in small groups, taking turns giving and following directions.

5 To practice a new set of sight words, white-out the street signs on a master copy of the map, fill in new sight word street names, and make copies.

Tip

Use the sight words on the map to teach other word recognition skills. For example, to introduce compound words, have students find See Saw Street. Ask: If you put the words *see* and *saw* together, what word do you make? (*seesaw*)

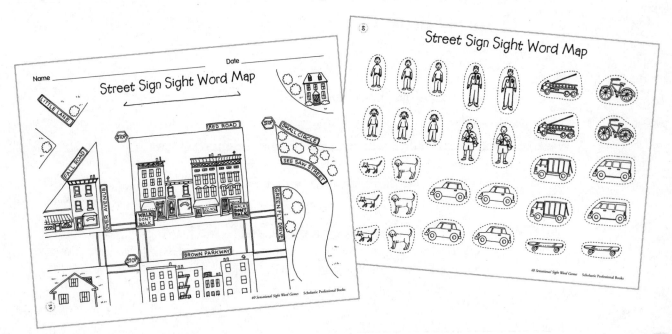

47

Sight Word Wheels

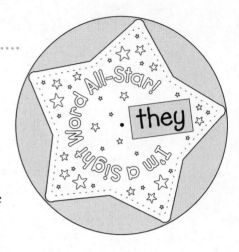

Use the patterns on pages 61 and 62 to make word wheels that will motivate children to practice reading and spelling one set of sight words. Then make new wheels to learn more.

1 Give each child a copy of the word wheel patterns. Have children decorate wheel A and cut out the window as indicated. Then have them write sight words to learn on the lines of wheel B.

2 Have them place wheel A on top of wheel B, then push a paper fastener through the center of both wheels. Show them how to open the two parts of the fastener and flatten them against the back of B.

3 Invite children to turn their wheels and read the words. Encourage them to help each other with words they don't know.

Picture Puzzles

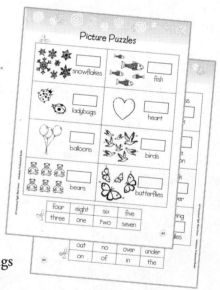

These mini-puzzles give early readers support with pictures and predictable text.

1 Give each child a copy of page 63.

2 Have children color the pictures and cut out the picture and word cards.

3 Read the "heart" puzzle together and ask children what word they think belongs in the space. Write "one" on the chalkboard. Have everyone find that word card and place it on the puzzle in the appropriate space. Read the phrase "one heart" together.

4 Let children continue on their own or with a partner. Read the phrases together, writing them on the chalkboard and letting children take turns underlining and saying the sight word.

Buzz!

Name _____ Date _____

Play-Clay Shape and Spell

Dear Families,

Use play clay and the letters on this page to make letter shapes and build words. First, cut apart the letters on the dashed lines. Then put them together to make any of these words:

_____.

Roll play-clay into "snakes." Use the play-clay snakes to fill in the letters. Read the words together!

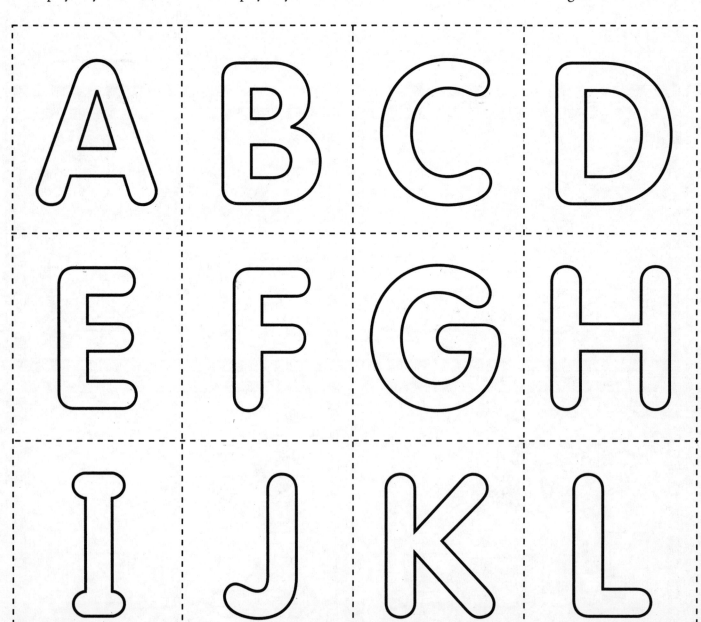

40 Sensational Sight Word Games Scholastic Professional Books

Play-Clay Shape and Spell

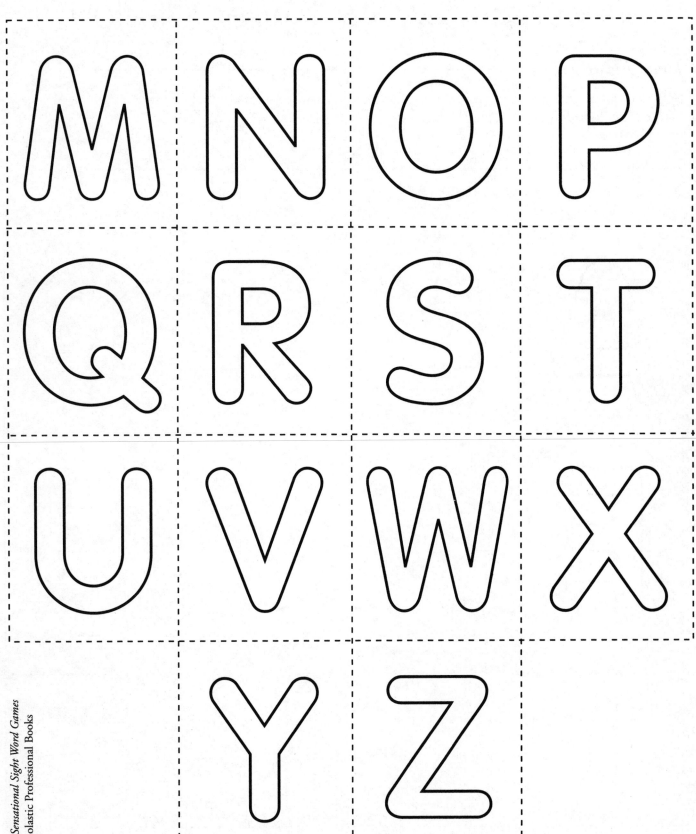

Peekaboo Word-Finder Window

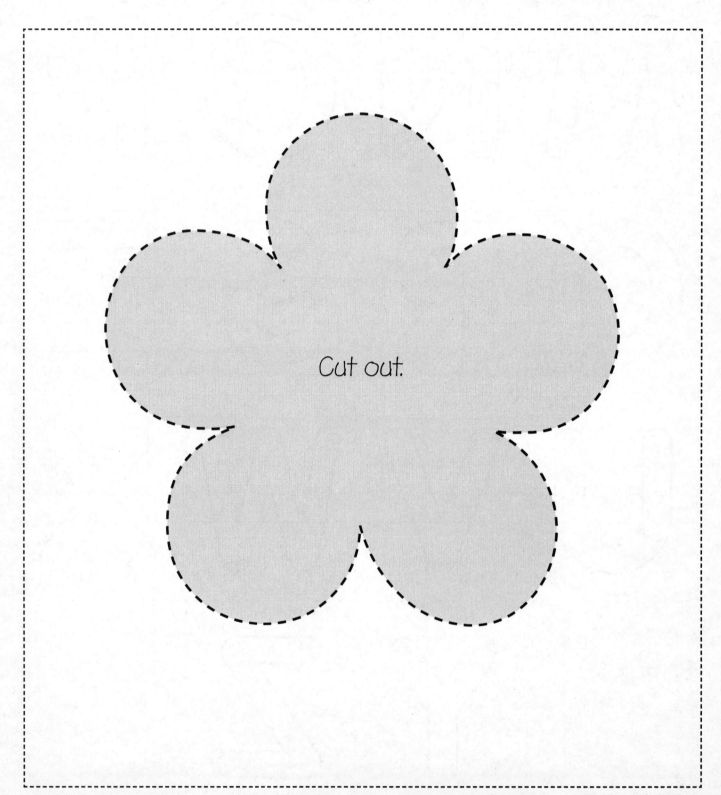

Cut out.

Sight Word Bingo

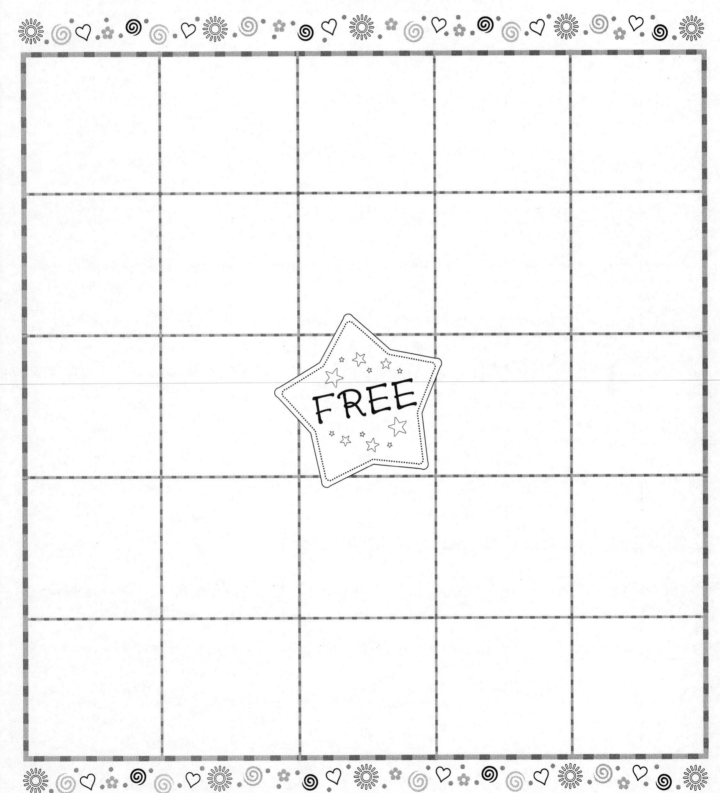

Sight Word Search

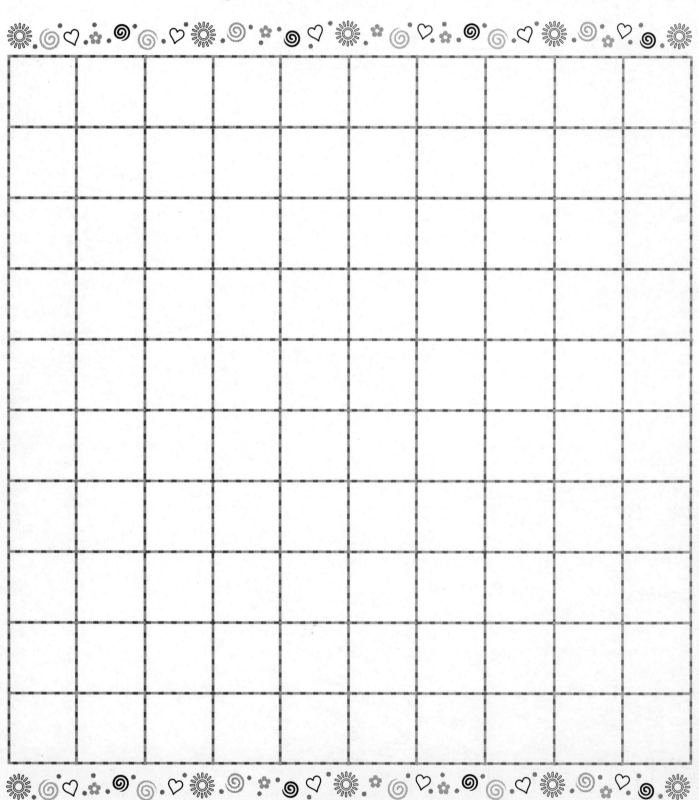

40 Sensational Sight Word Games Scholastic Professional Books

Grow a
Sight Word
Garden

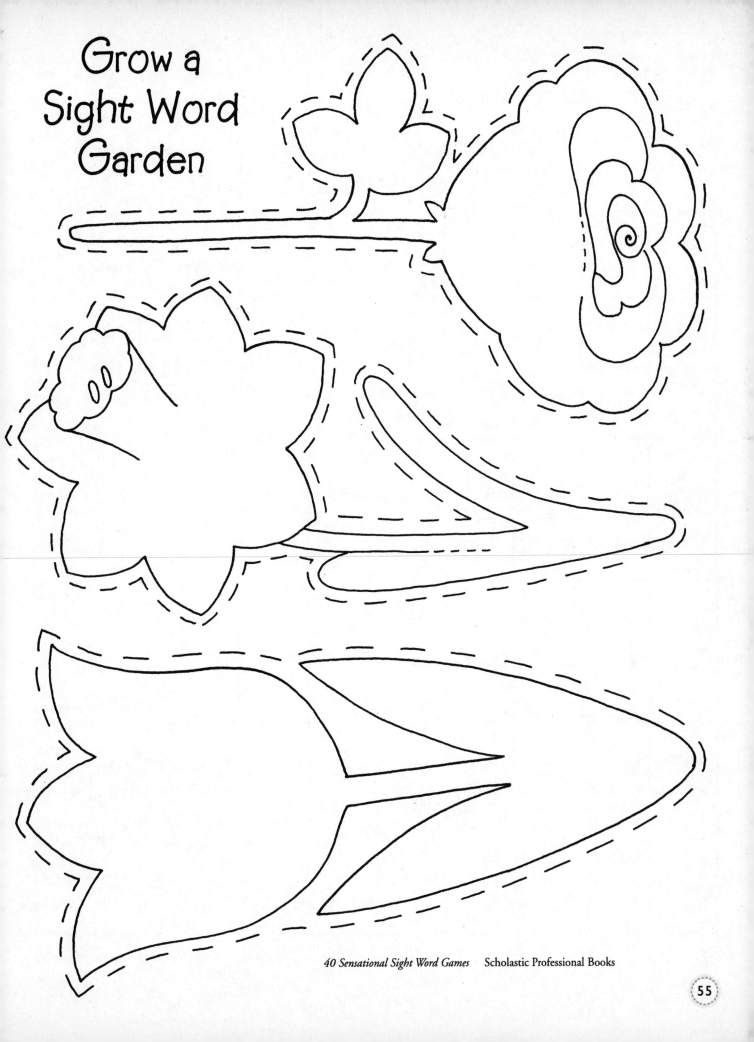

Word Construction Site

Look at the letters in this crane. Use them to complete all of the words in the bricks on the building.

Zoom!

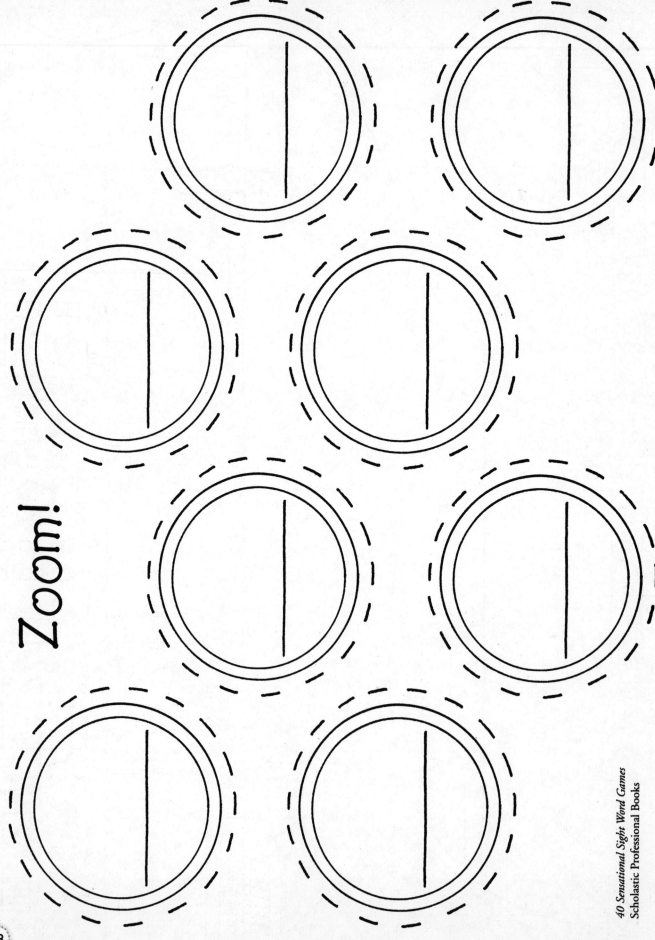

Zoom!

40 Sensational Sight Word Games
Scholastic Professional Books

Name _____

Date _____

Street Sign Sight Word Map

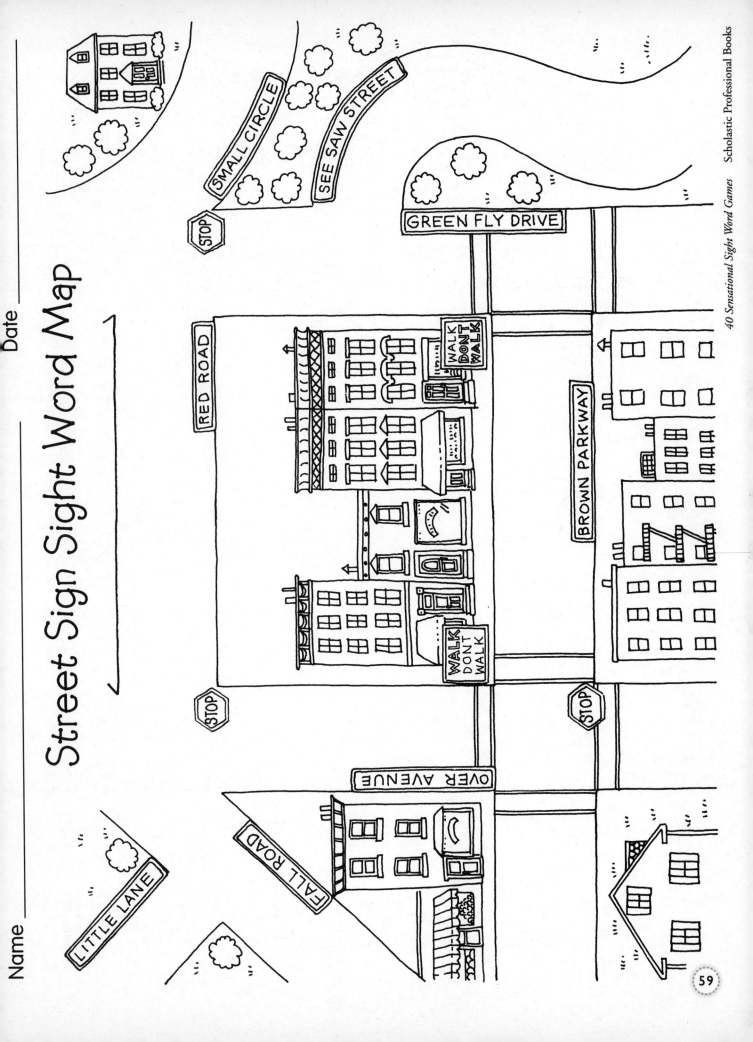

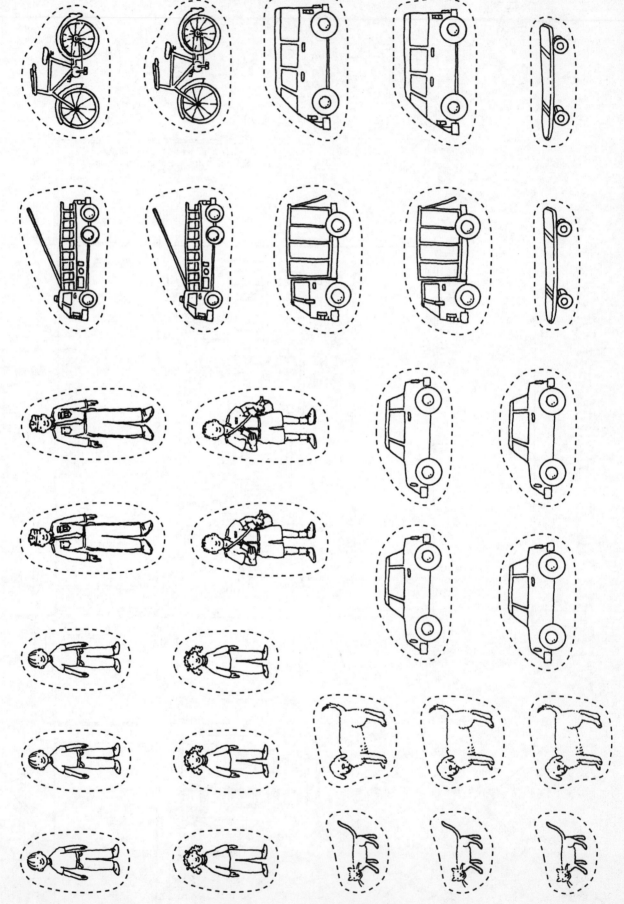

Street Sign Sight Word Map

40 Sensational Sight Word Games   Scholastic Professional Books

All-Star Sight Word Wheel

Wheel A

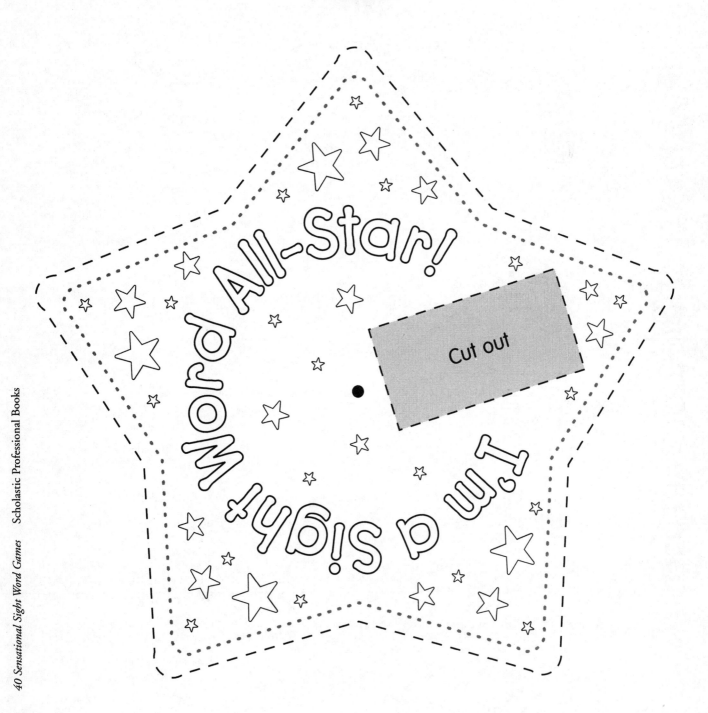

Word All-Star!

I'm a Sight Word

Cut out

All-Star Sight Word Wheel

Wheel B

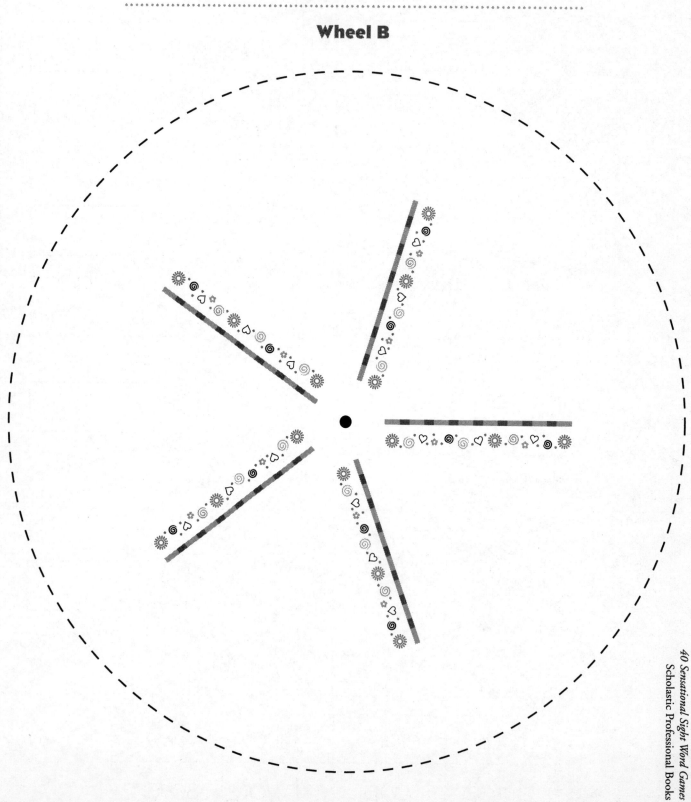

40 Sensational Sight Word Games
Scholastic Professional Books

Picture Puzzles

 snowflakes

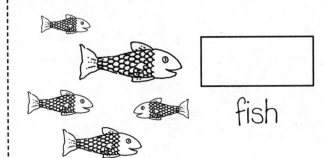 fish

 ladybugs

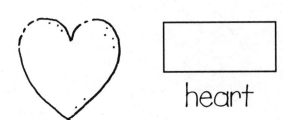 heart

 balloons

 birds

 bears

 butterflies

four	eight	six	five
three	one	two	seven

Picture Puzzles

cat

a tree

glass

milk

put

a hat

the
moon

the
bed

pick

flower

more
cereal

blowing

candles

out	no	over	under
on	of	in	the